SPECTRUM® READERS

LEVEL 2

W9-AWQ-239

TOUR!
North America

By Lisa Kurkov

Carson-Dellosa Publishing

An imprint of Carson-Dellosa Publishing, LLC
P.O. Box 35665
Greensboro, NC 27425-5665

carsondellosa.com

Printed in the USA. All rights reserved.
ISBN 978-1-4838-0124-7

01-002141120

North America is vast.
It is made up of 23 countries.
It stretches all the way from Canada
to Panama.
Some things that make it special were
made by humans.
Others are natural.
Let's tour the continent from north to
south.

Baffin Island

First on the tour is Baffin Island.
It is found in northeast Canada, in the icy Arctic Ocean.
The island lies between Greenland and the mainland of Canada.
Its mountains are full of glaciers.
Polar bears and walruses live here.

Yukon River

Next on the tour is the Yukon River.
Its chilly waters flow through Alaska
and northwest Canada.
Tall mountains surround the river.
Russian explorers traveled to the Yukon.
People came here looking for gold.

Quebec

Next on the tour is Quebec.
This area of Canada is home to the
castle Le Château Frontenac (sha TOE
FRUN tuh nak).
It has 618 rooms!
French settlers founded Quebec, and
people here still speak French today.

British Columbia

Next on the tour is British Columbia. In this part of western Canada, rugged mountains overlook the Pacific Ocean. Foggy islands can be seen off the coast. Huge ships dock in the city of Vancouver.

12

Rocky Mountains

Next on the tour are the Rocky Mountains.
These tall, jagged peaks run through Canada and the United States.
The Continental Divide is an imaginary line through the Rockies.
On one side, water flows east.
On the other side, water flows west.

New England

Next on the tour is New England.
Settlers from England first came to this part of the northeast U.S.
Lighthouses and fishing boats line the rocky Atlantic coast.
Small villages in Maine and Rhode Island are here.
The big city of Boston is here, too.

New York City

Next on the tour is New York City.
It is the largest city in the U.S.
Over eight million people live here!
Skyscrapers tower over busy city streets.
New York City is called "the city that
never sleeps."

St. Louis, Missouri

Next on the tour is St. Louis.
This city in the midwest U.S. is home to
the Gateway Arch.
It is 63 stories tall and stands on the
banks of the Mississippi River.
St. Louis was the "gateway" to the west
for pioneers.

Yellowstone Park

Next on the tour is Yellowstone National Park.

It is found in Wyoming, Montana, and Idaho.

Here, lava heats water underground.

Hot water shoots from geysers and bubbles in pools.

Bacteria in Morning Glory Pool make its bright colors.

The Grand Canyon

Next on the tour is the Grand Canyon. Visitors to the Arizona desert come to see this amazing sight.
The canyon is a mile deep in some places!
The Colorado River carved its steep walls over millions of years.

San Francisco, California

Next on the tour is San Francisco.
Here, the Golden Gate Bridge spans
San Francisco Bay.
Some people crossed the continent to
settle here, and others traveled across
the Pacific Ocean.
Many came in search of gold.

Mexico City

Next on the tour is Mexico City.
It is the capital of Mexico.
Over 600 years ago, the Aztecs built
a city in this same place.
Today, the modern city is home to
almost nine million people.

Chichén Itzá

Next on the tour is Chichén Itzá.
This ancient city stands on Mexico's
Yucatán Peninsula.
Here, people visit a Mayan pyramid.
Each of its four sides has 91 steps, plus
one step on top.
That makes 365 steps—one for each
day of the year!

Chiapas, Mexico

Last on the tour is Chiapas.
This Mexican state is near the bottom
of the continent.
The beautiful Agua Azul waterfall is
found in a rain forest here.
Its name means "blue water."
Minerals make the water bright blue.

TOUR! North America
Comprehension Questions

1. How many countries are in North America?

2. How did the Gateway Arch get its name?

3. What is special about the pyramid in Chichén Itzá?

4. What river formed the Grand Canyon?

5. In what ocean is Baffin Island?

6. Why is the water of Agua Azul so blue?

7. Who explored the Yukon River?

8. Name three countries on the North American continent.

9. What is the capital of Mexico?

10. What is the Continental Divide? Can you see it?

11. What oceans border North America?